This Book Belongs To

_____

_____

Copyright 2022 Acts 10.1 Books
Jobos101 is Trademarked by: Jahlyric Boldini Designs, Llc
www.Jobos101.com

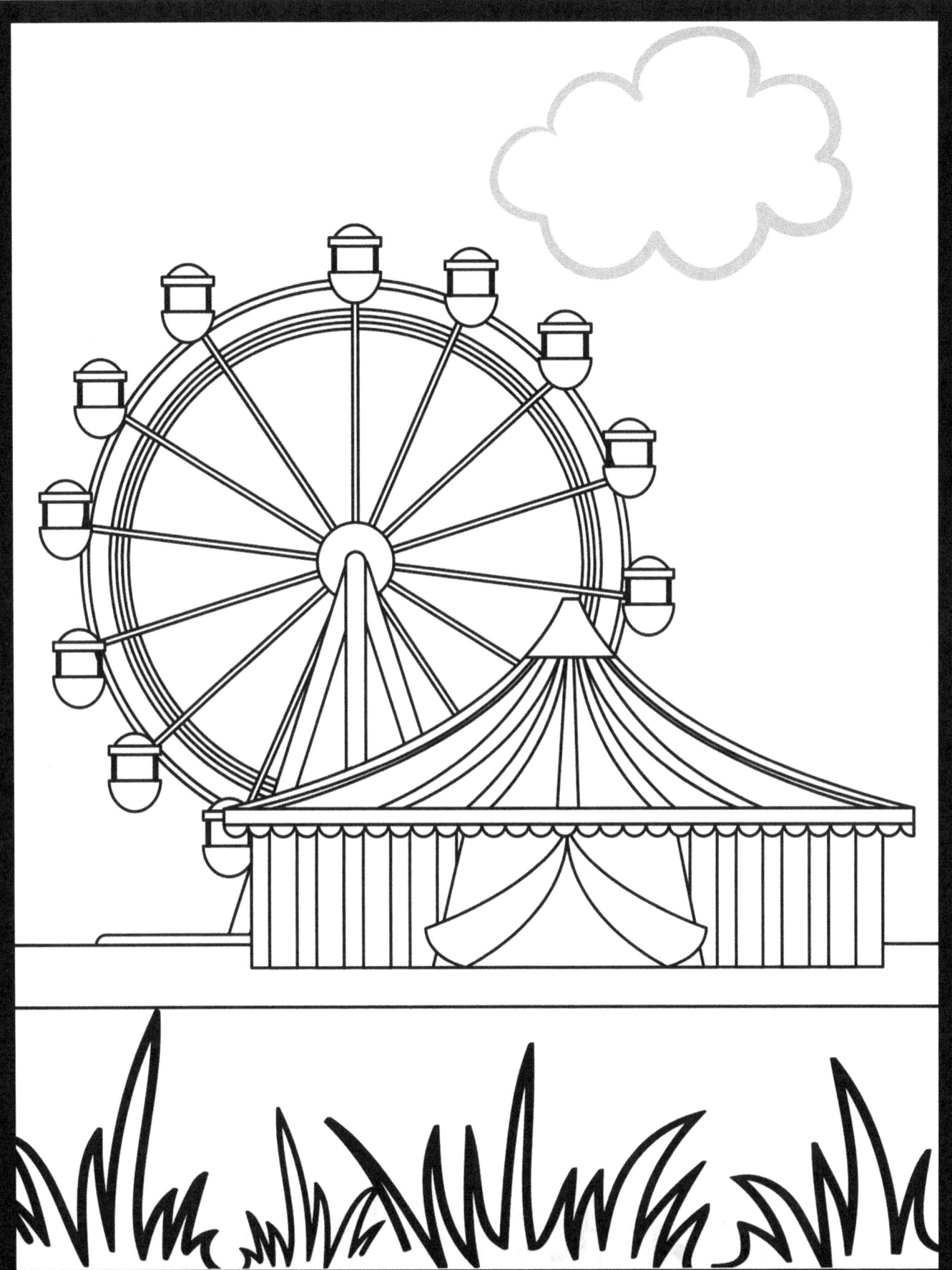

Relaxation

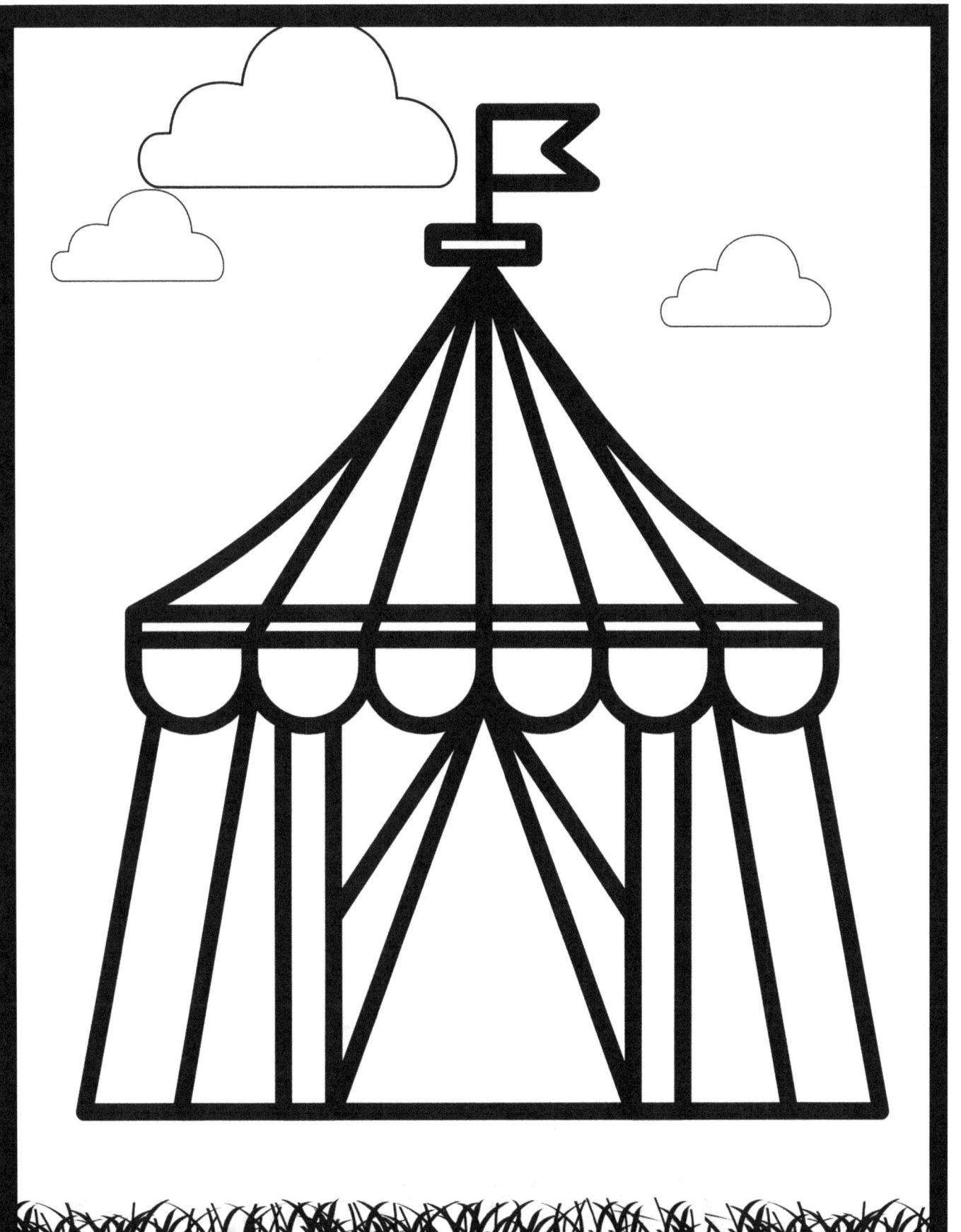

Chill Zone

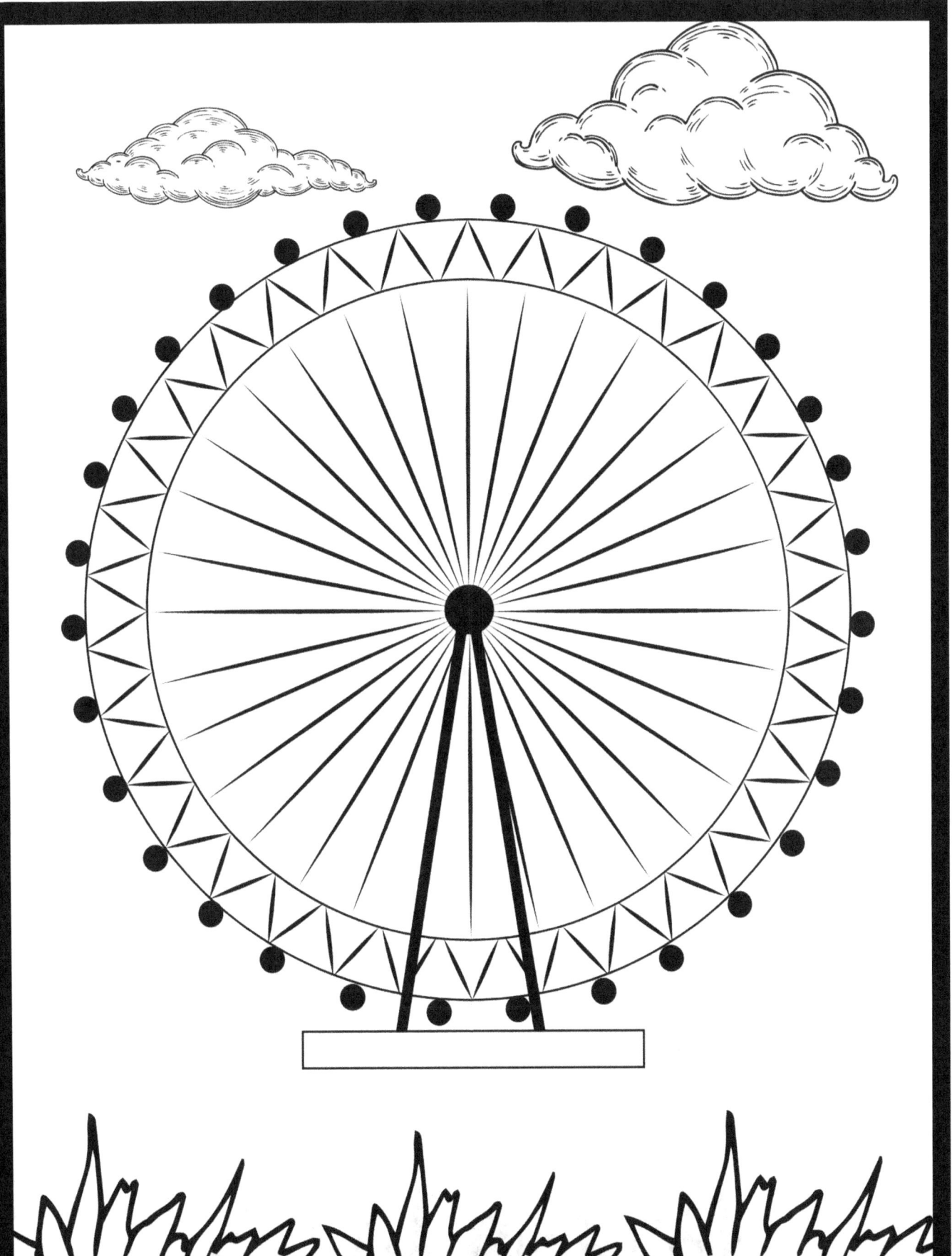

Circus Days

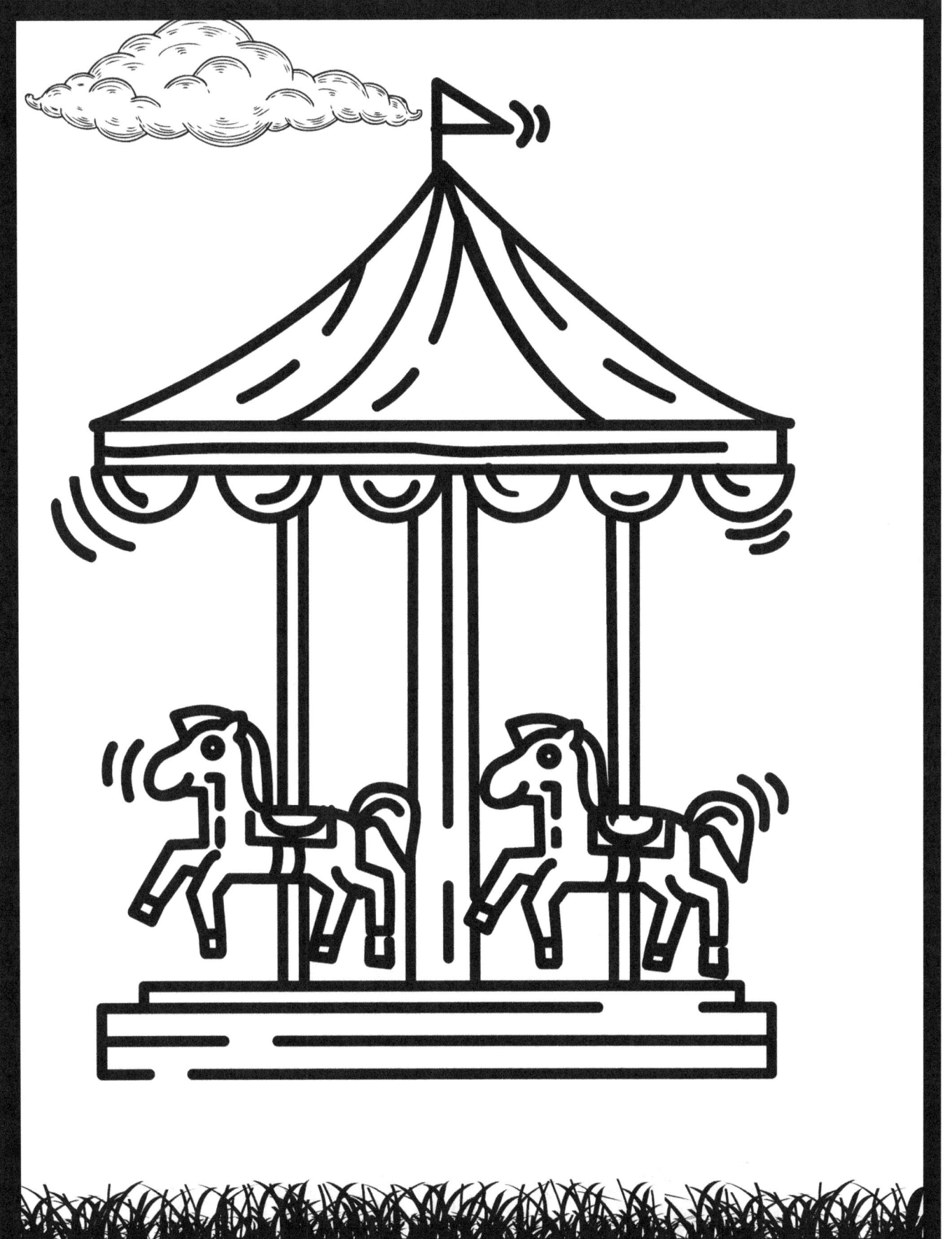

Take a Chance

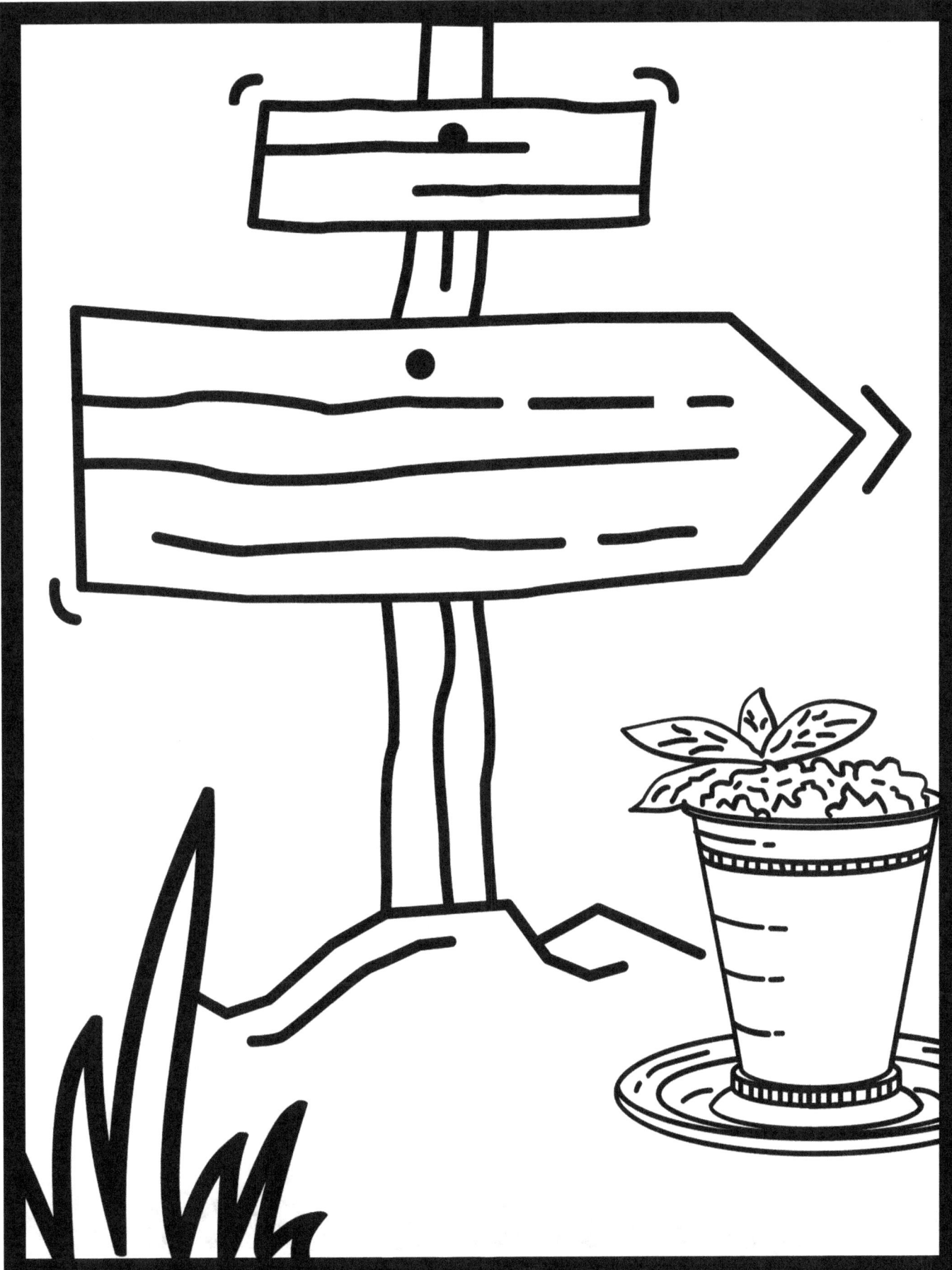

Take a Deep Breath

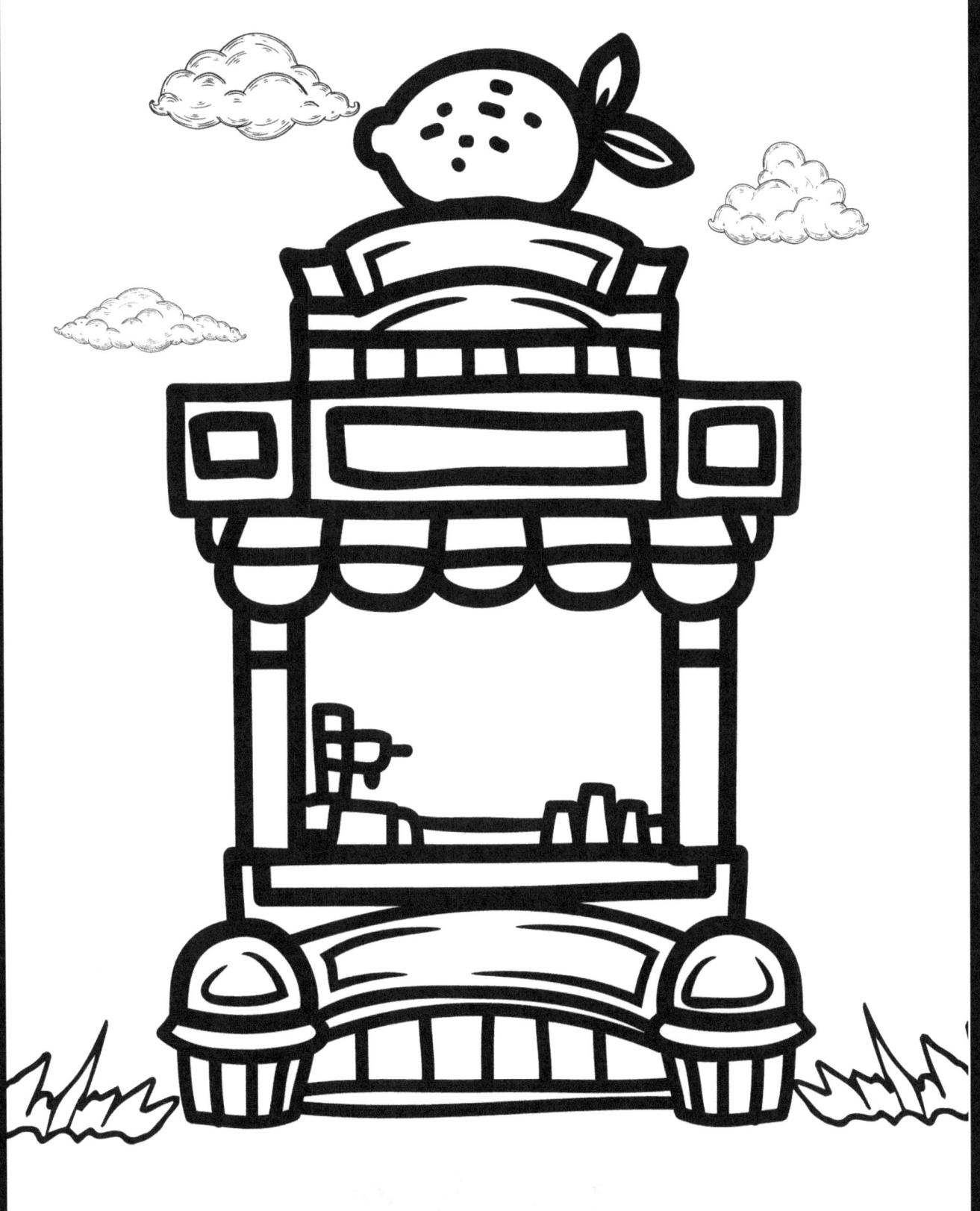

Smile

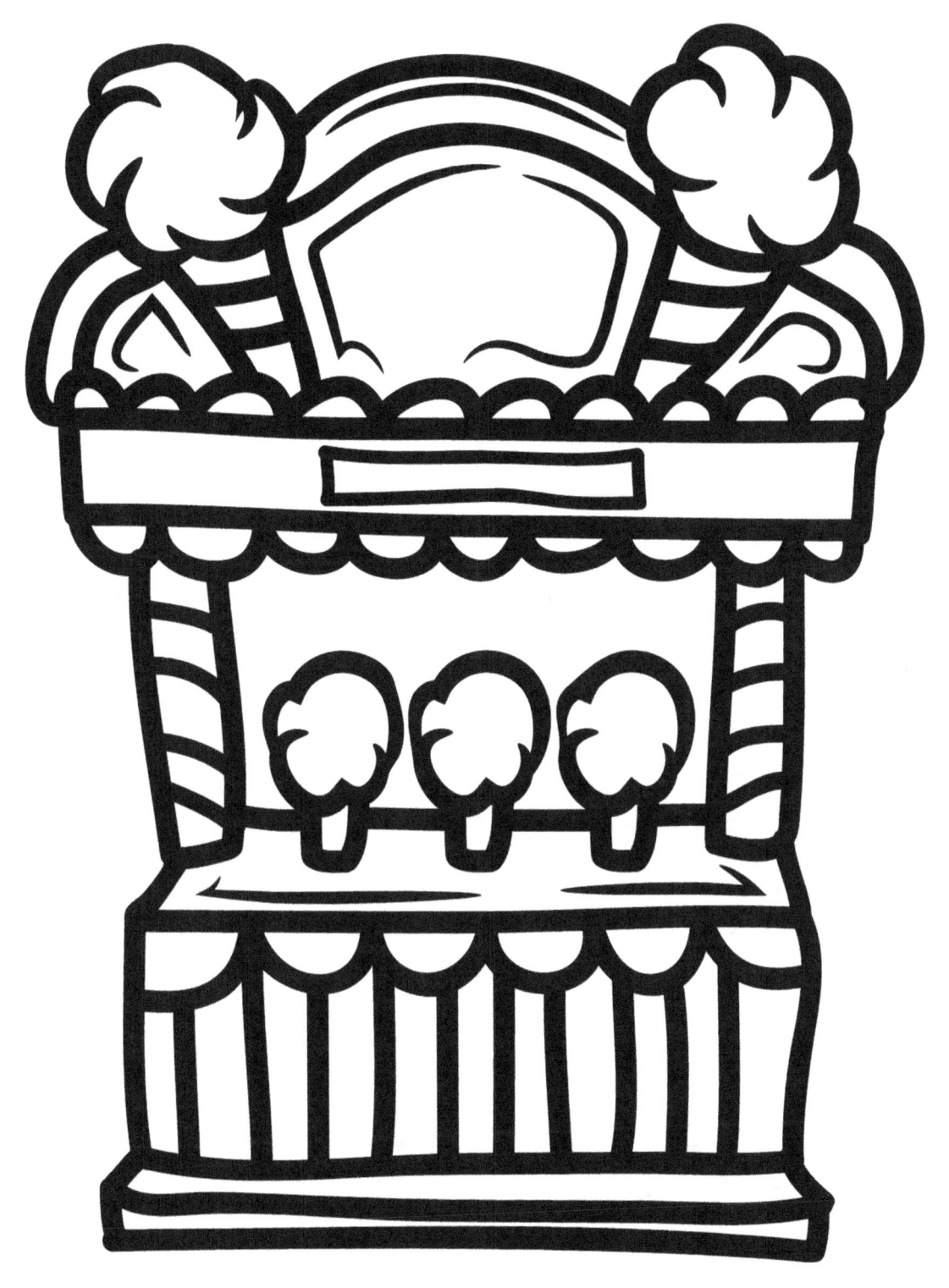

Lounge

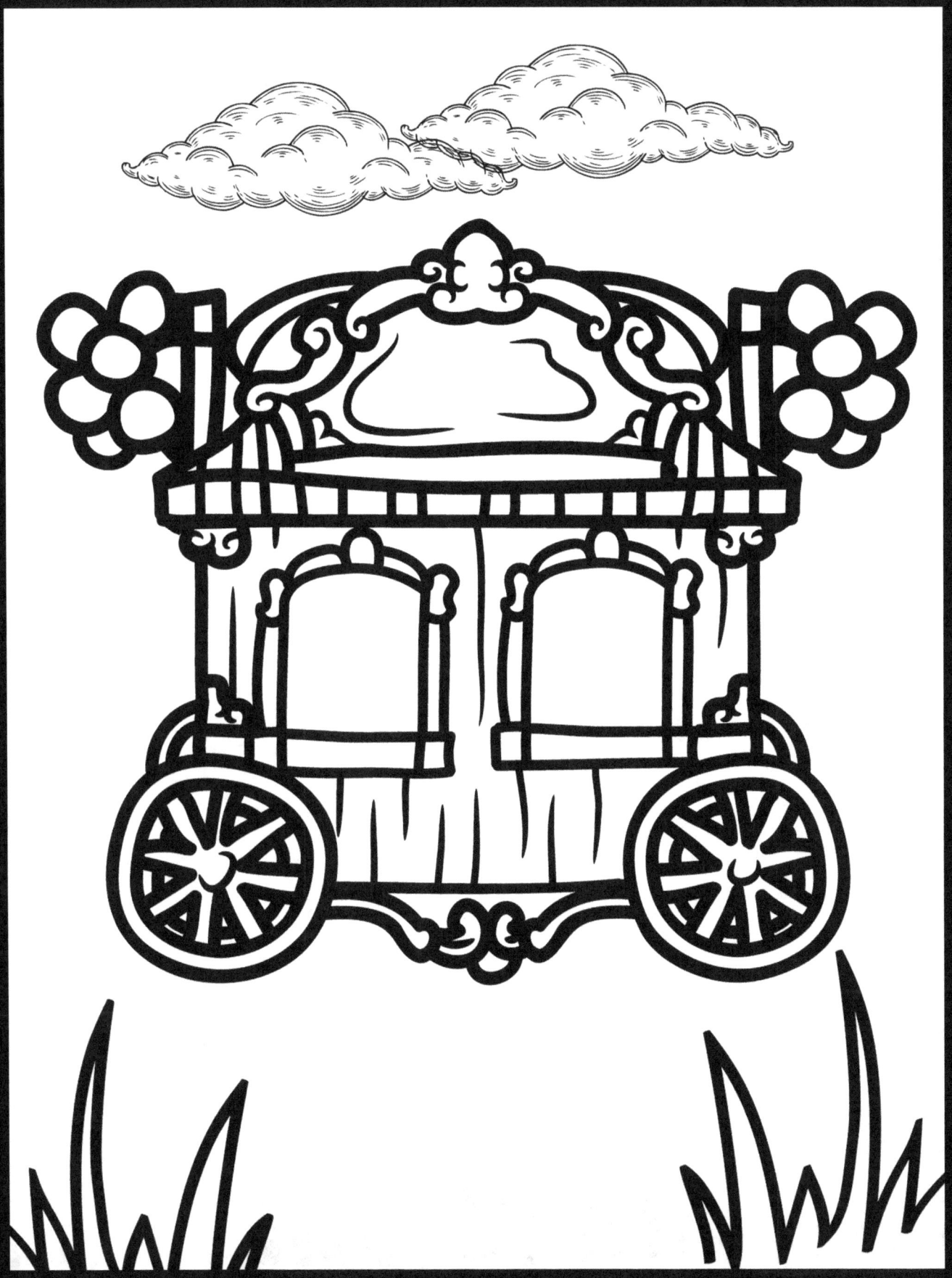

Chill Out

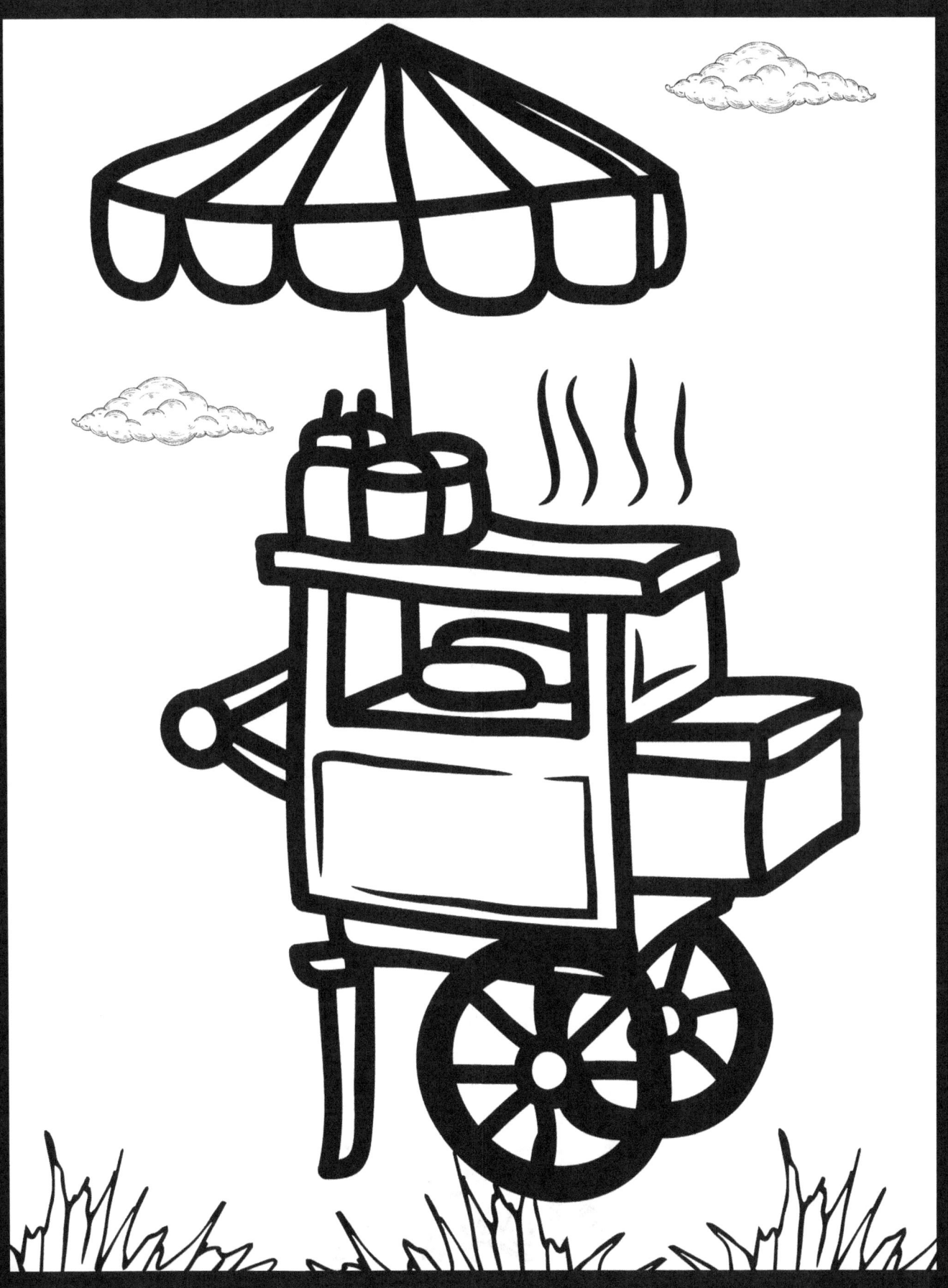

Relax

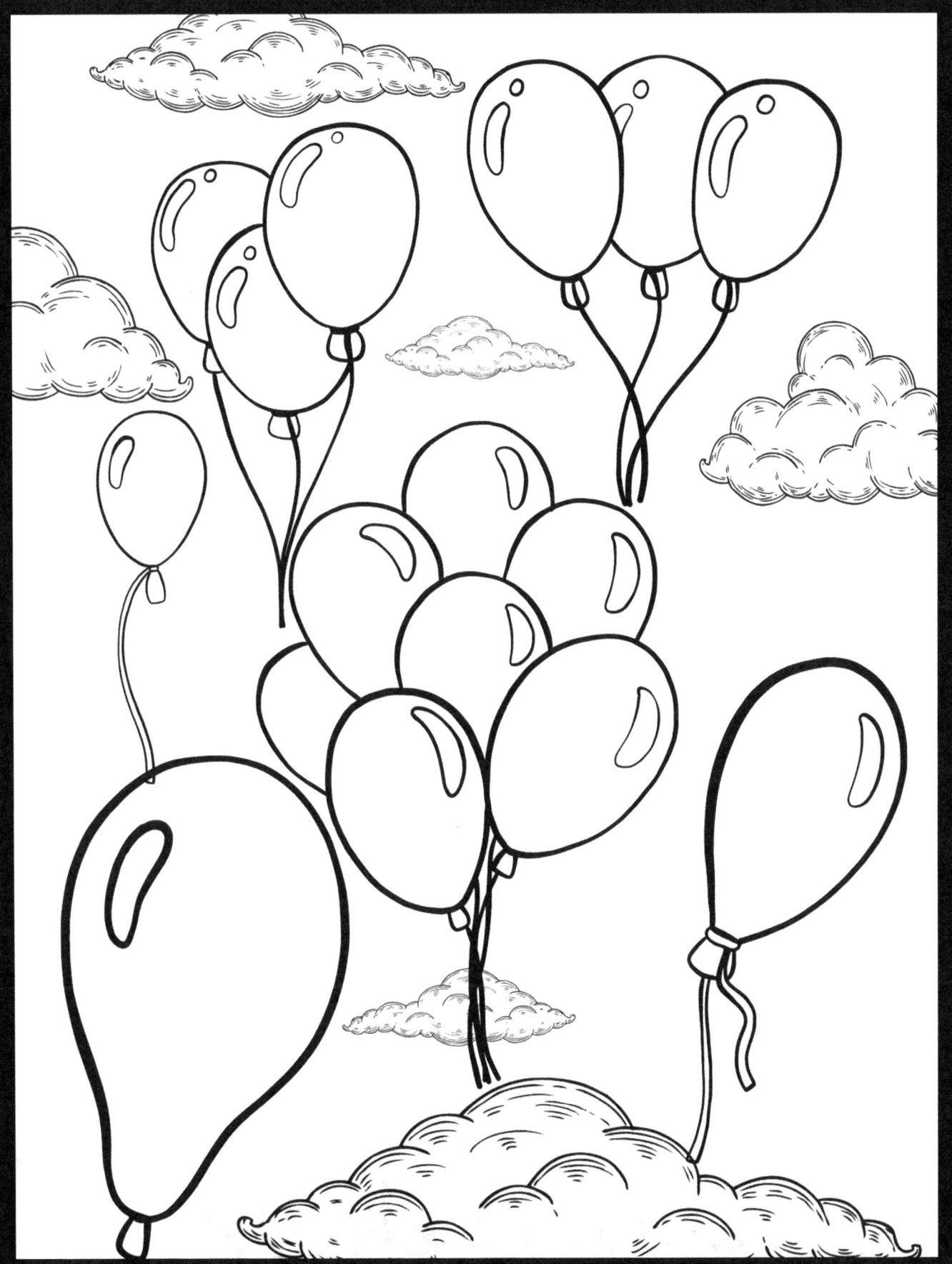

Circus Days

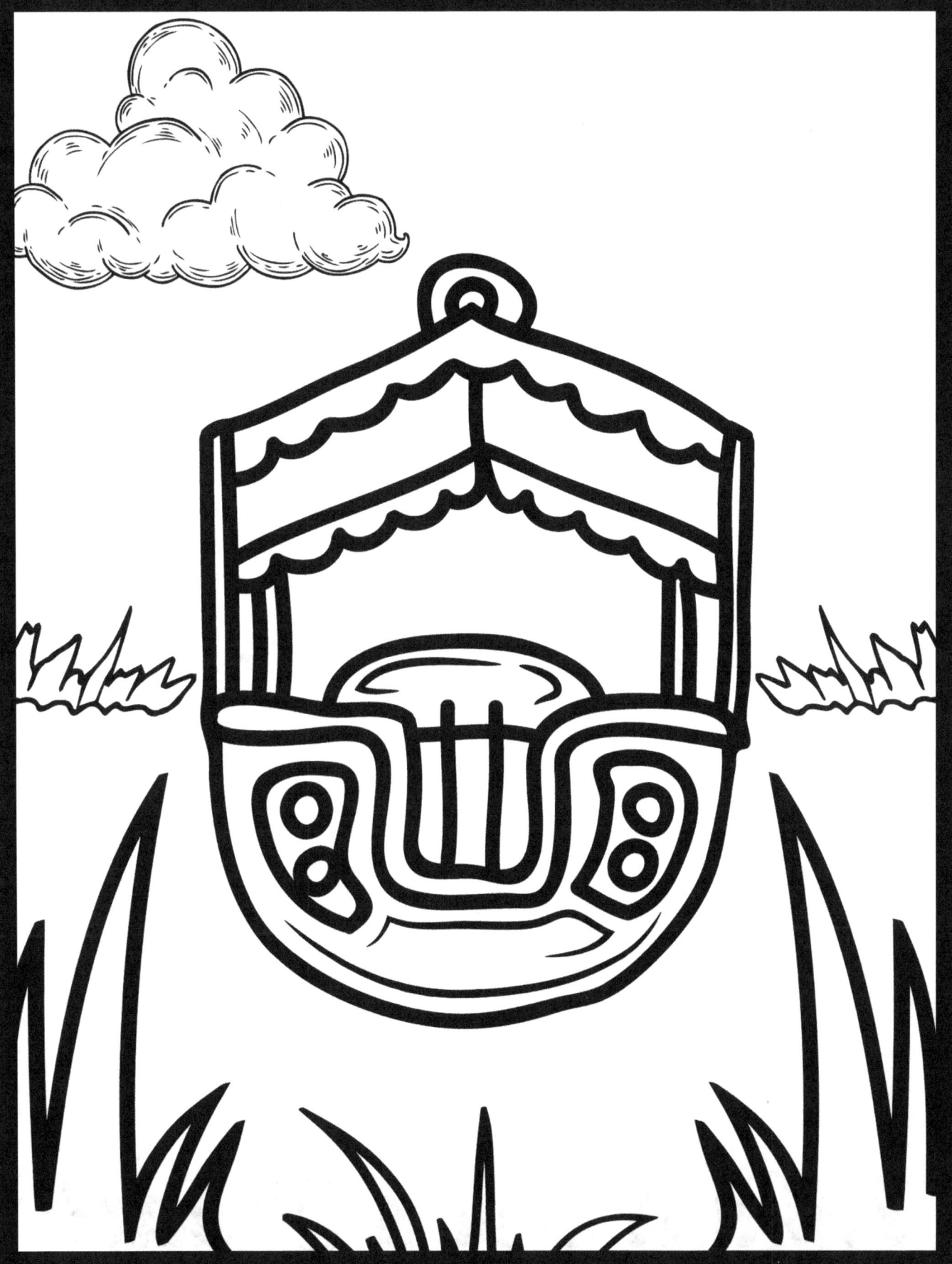

Take a Deep Breath

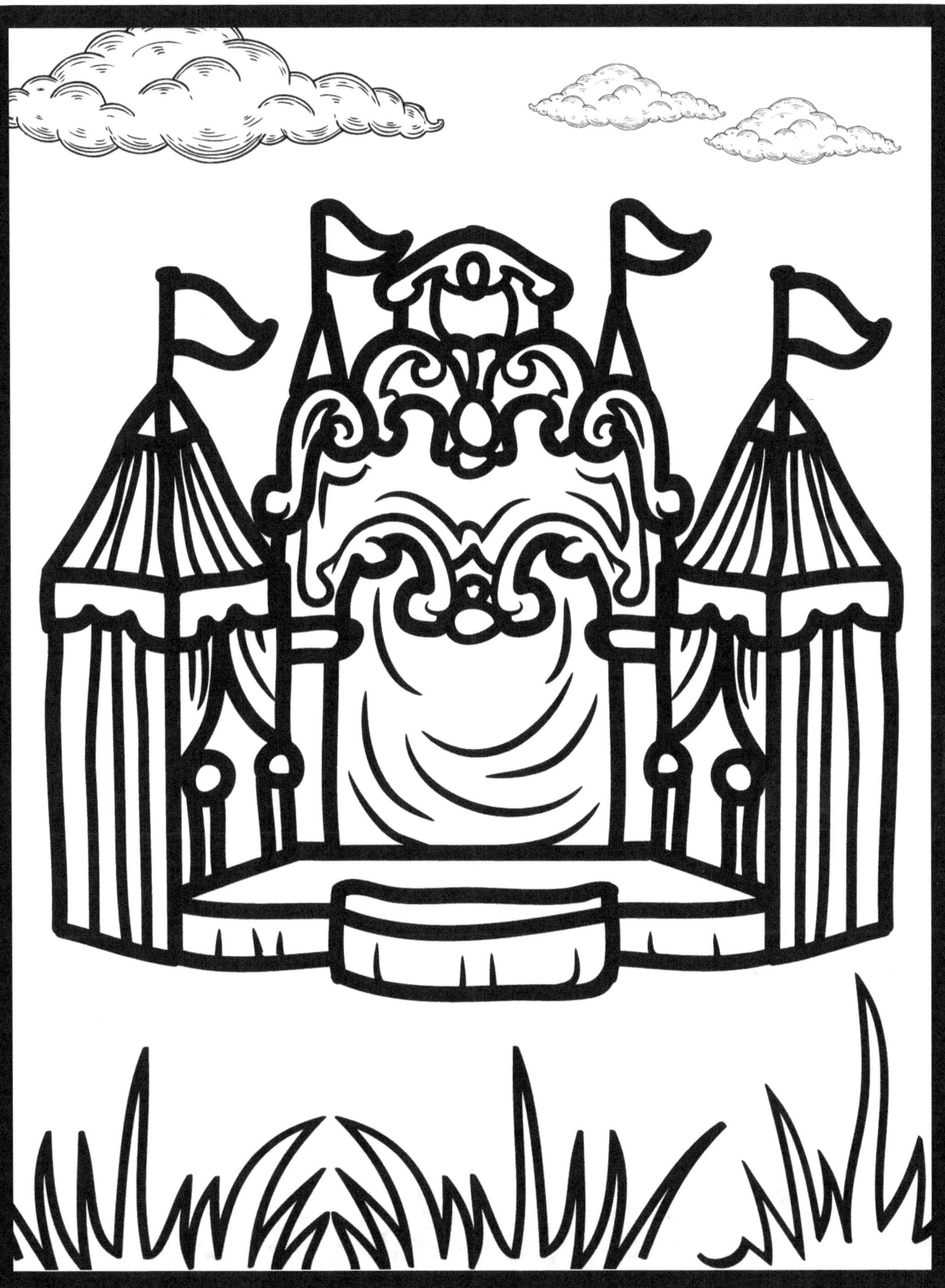

Take a Chance

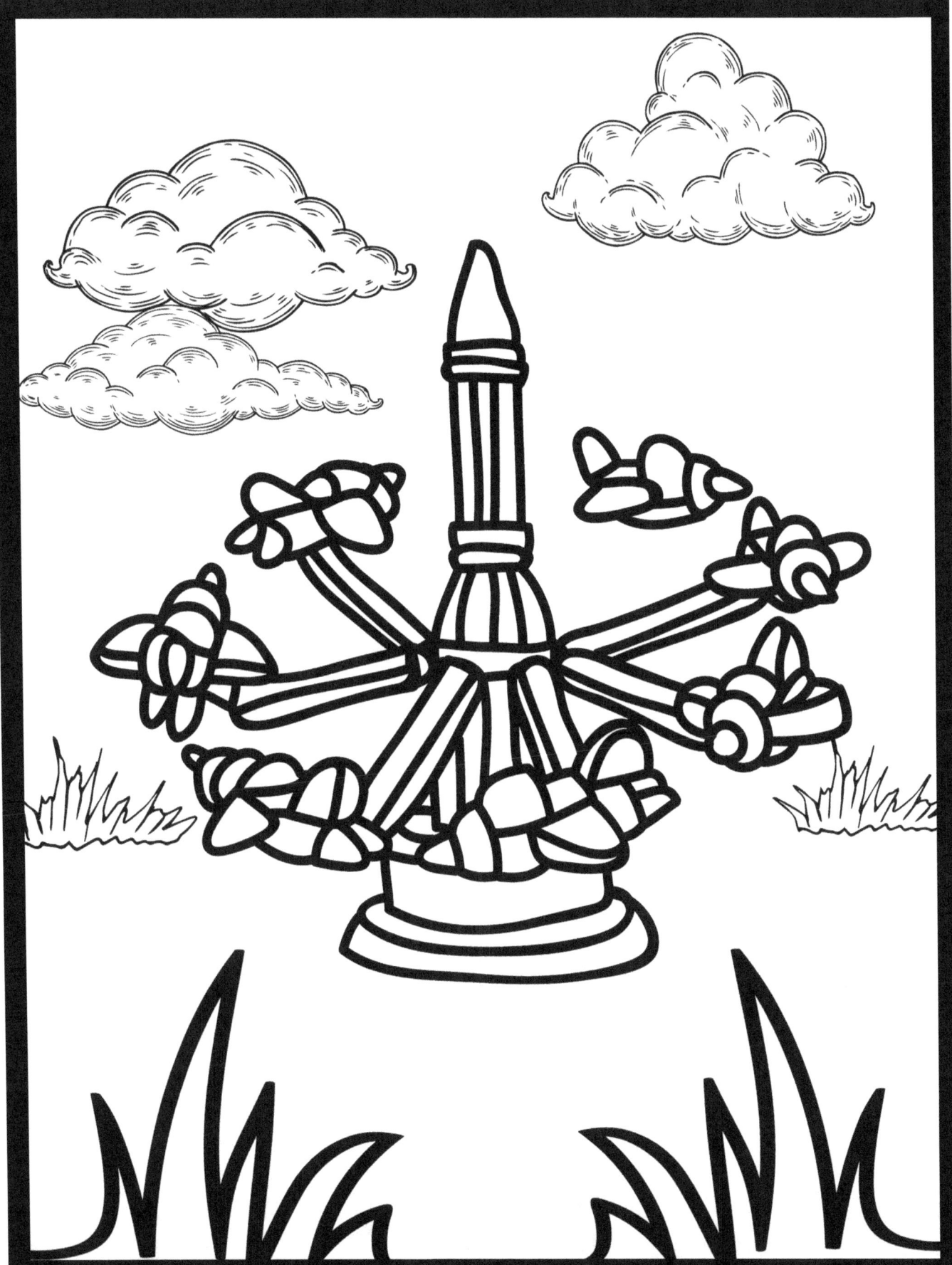

Smile

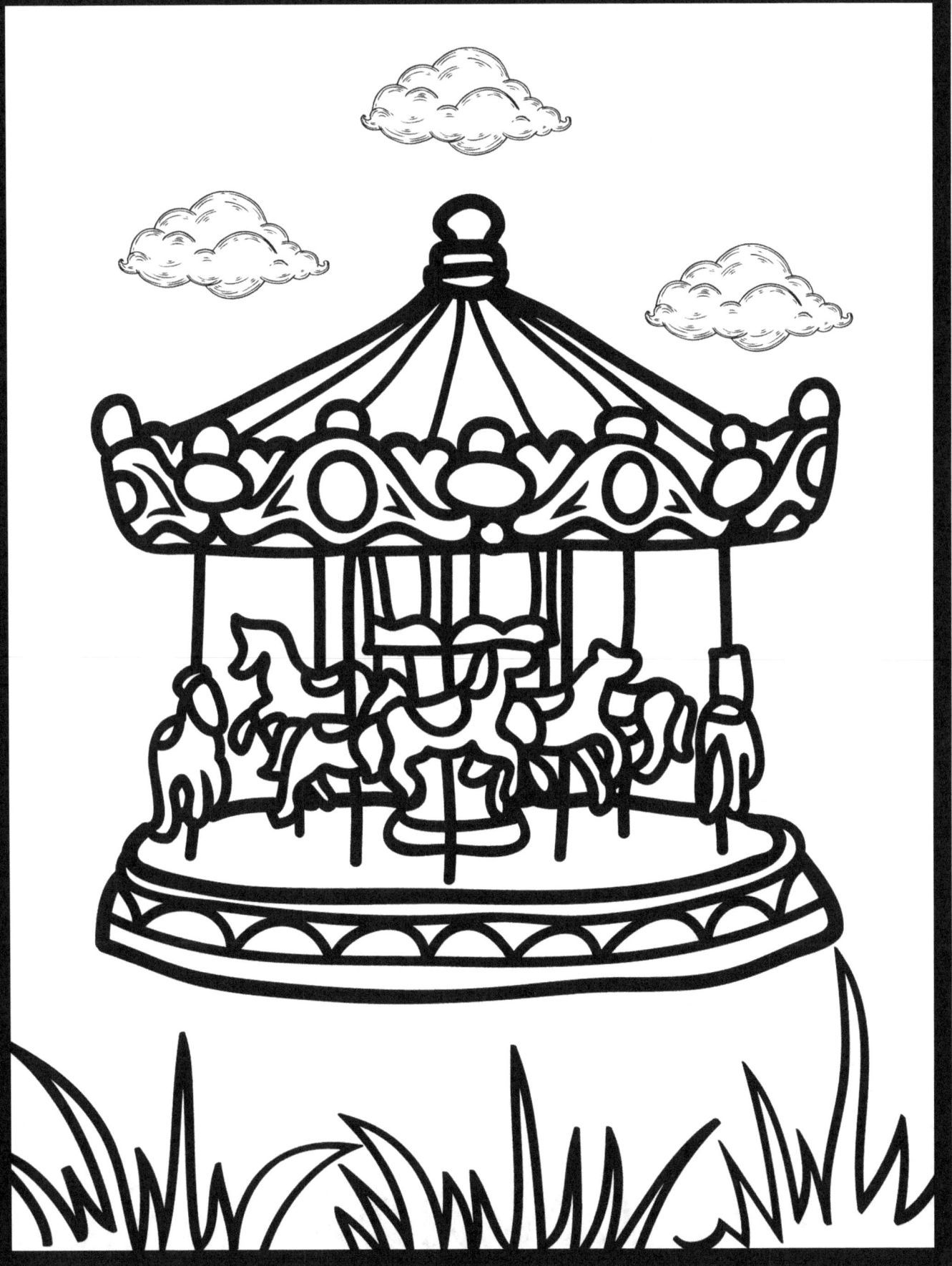

Lounge

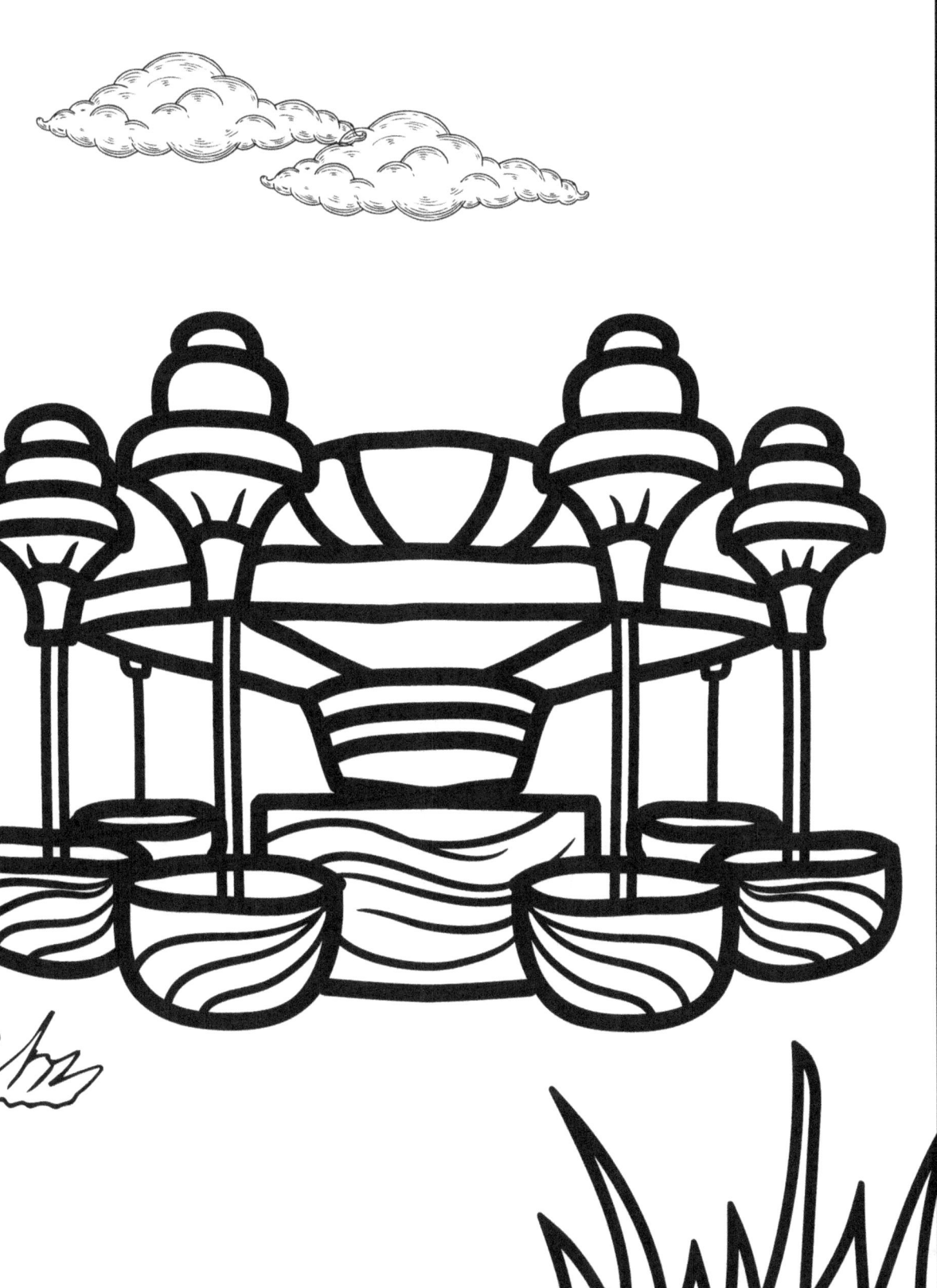

Chill Out

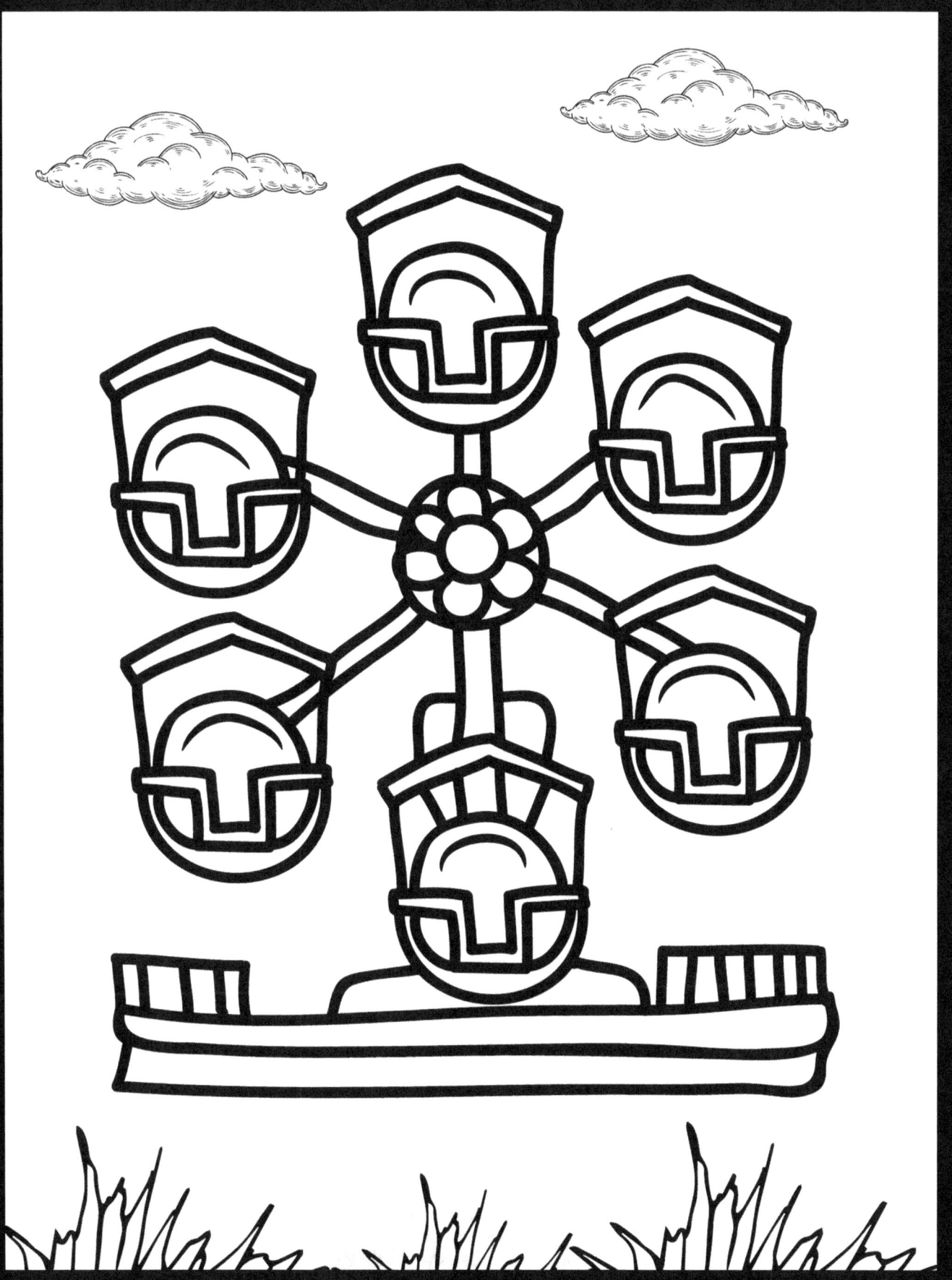

Relax

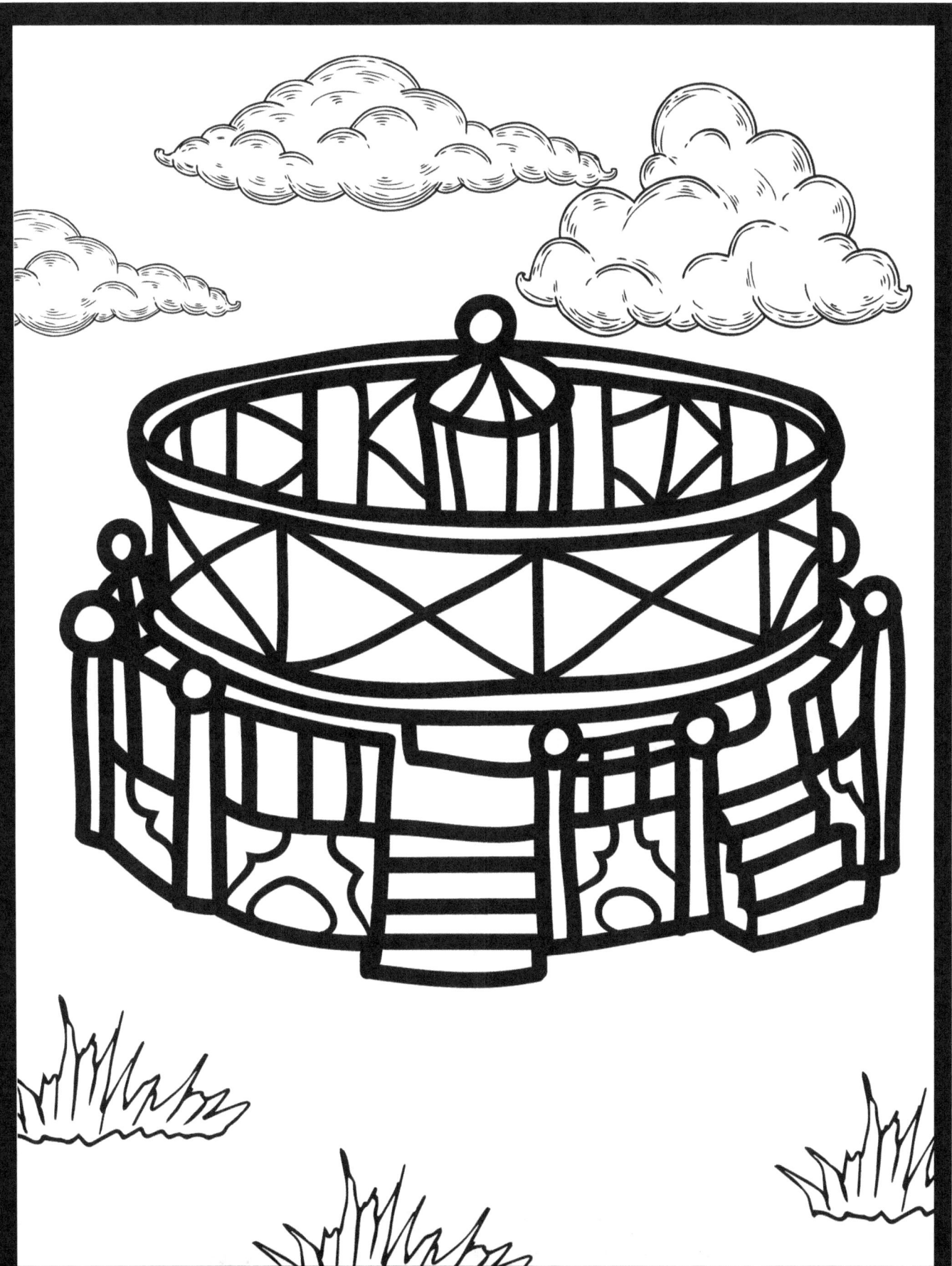

Circus Days

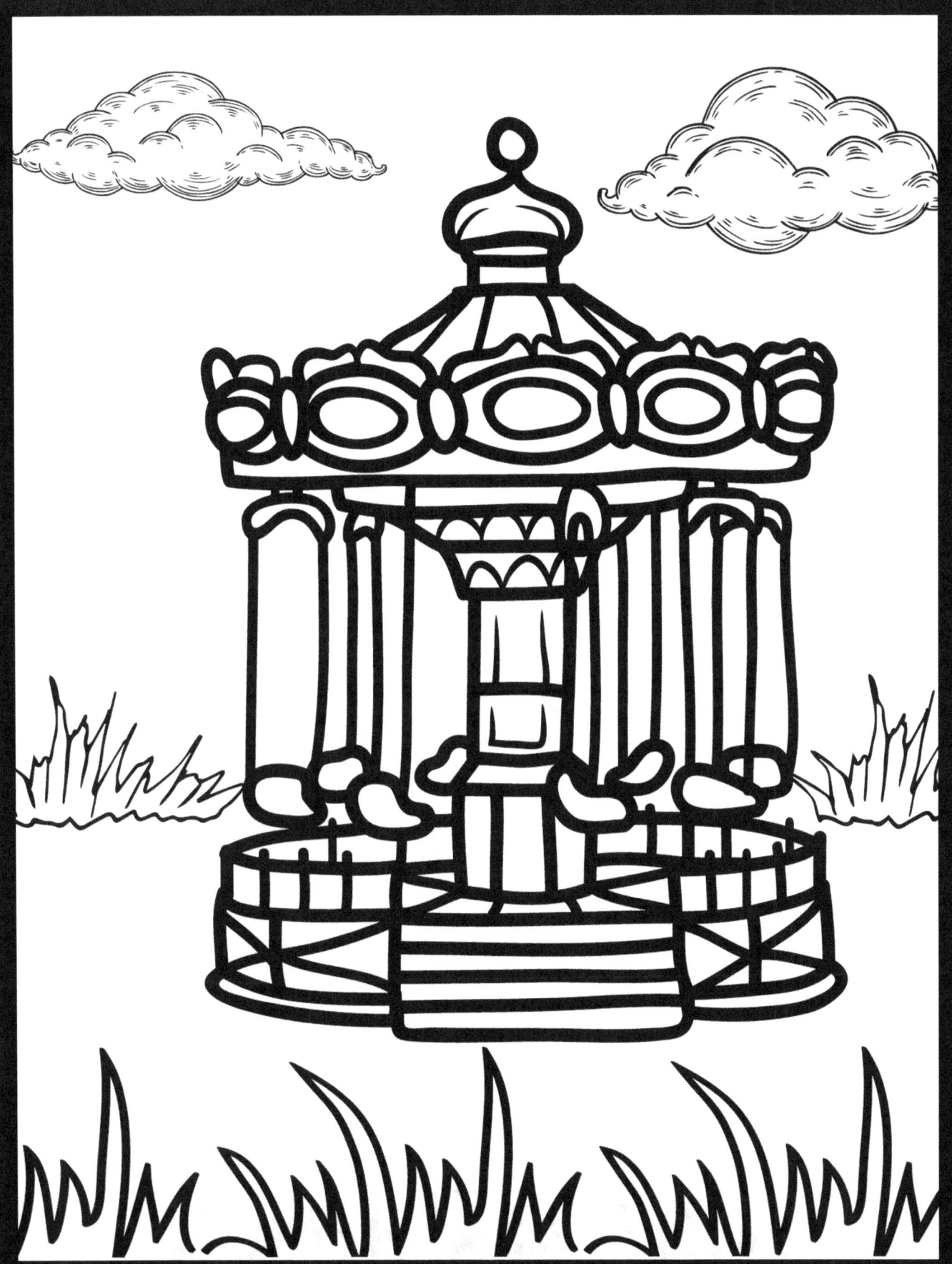

Take a Chance

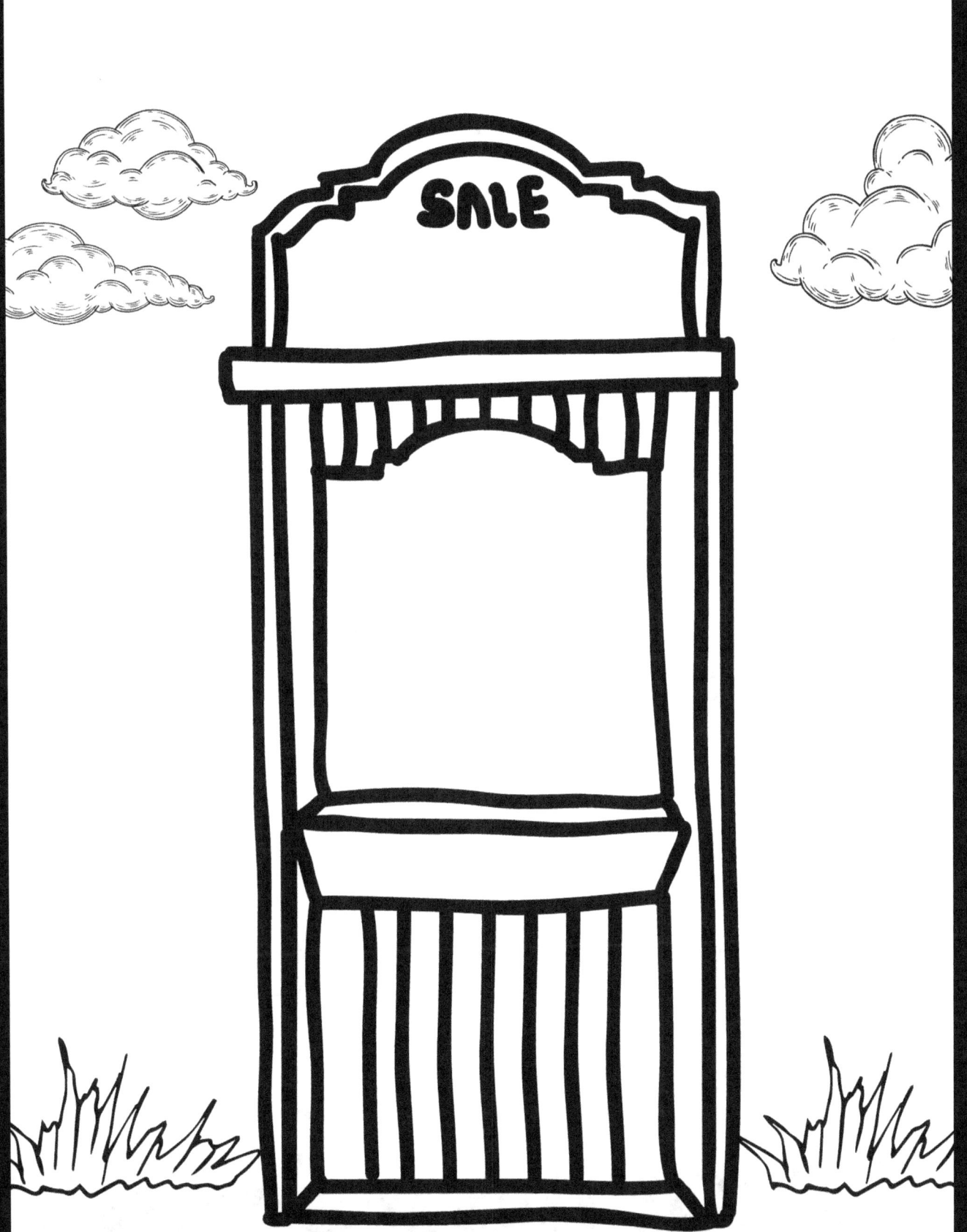

Take a deep Breath

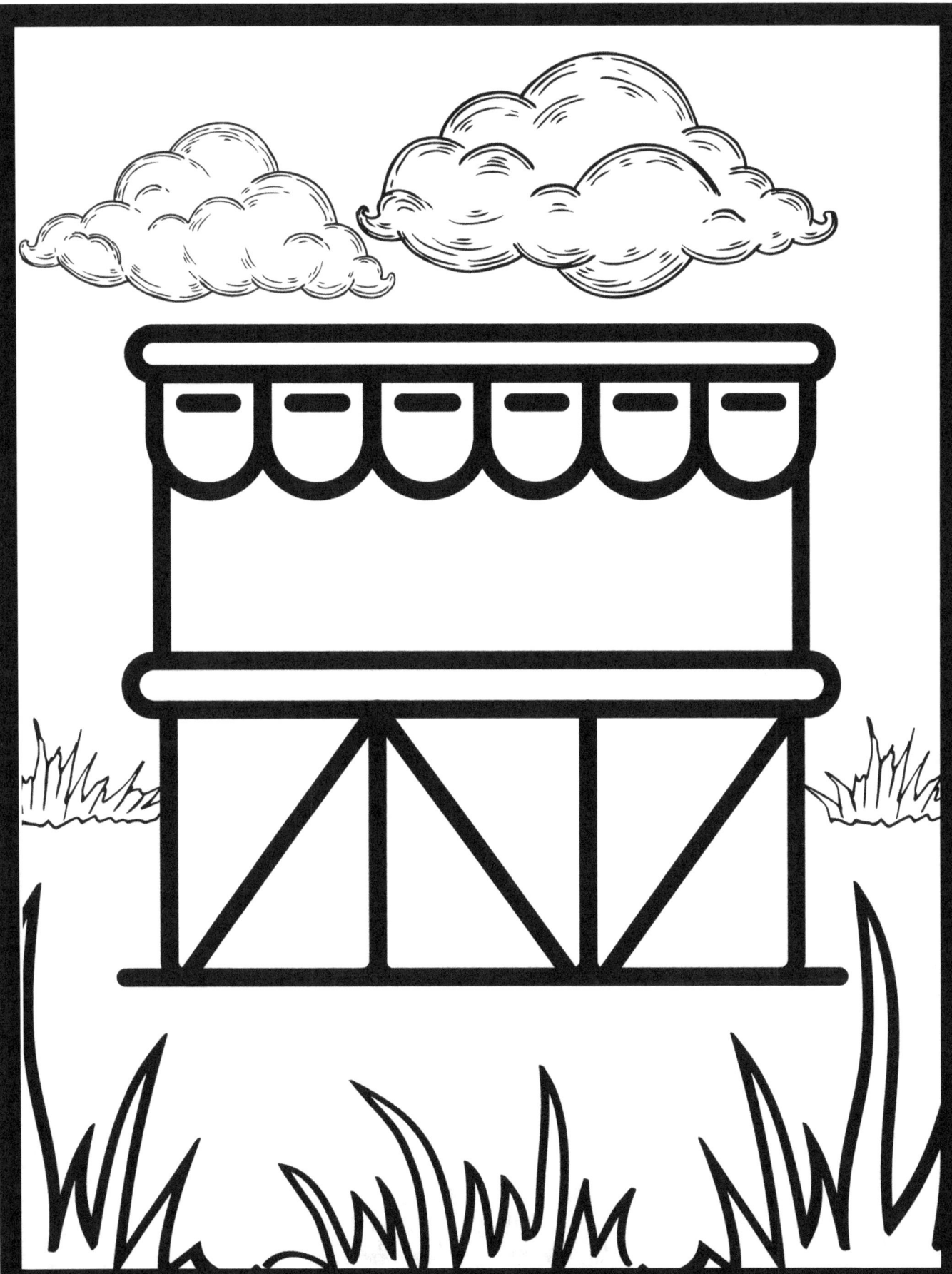

Smile

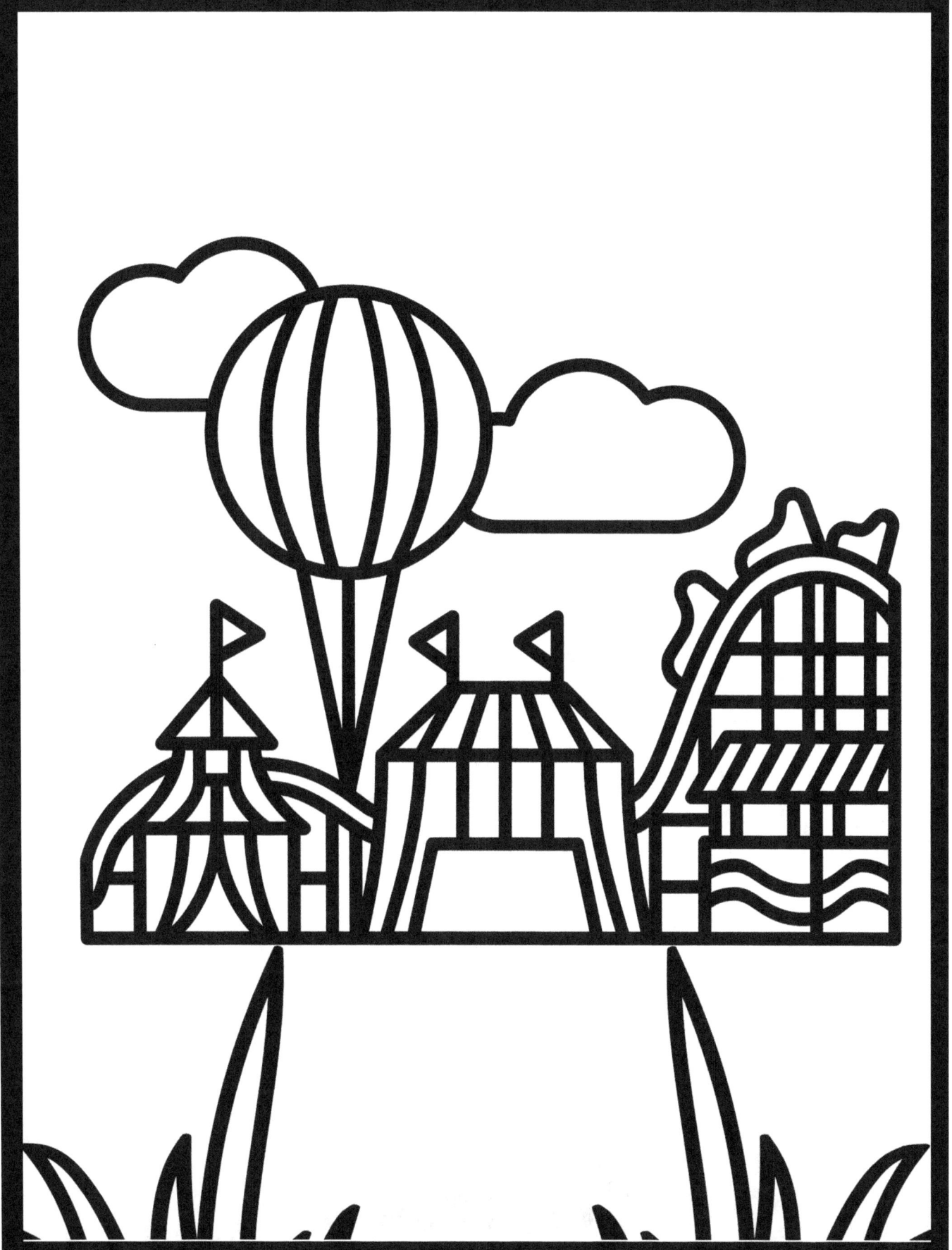

Lounge

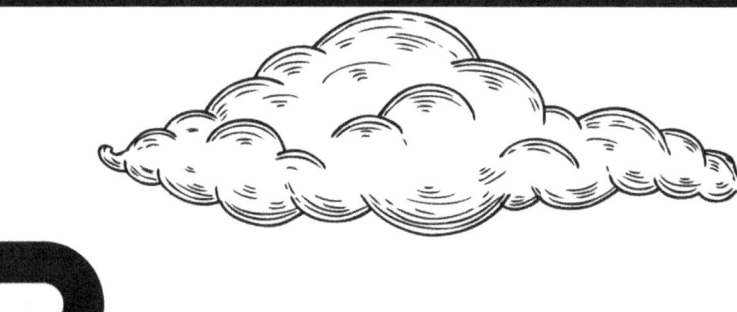

Chill Out

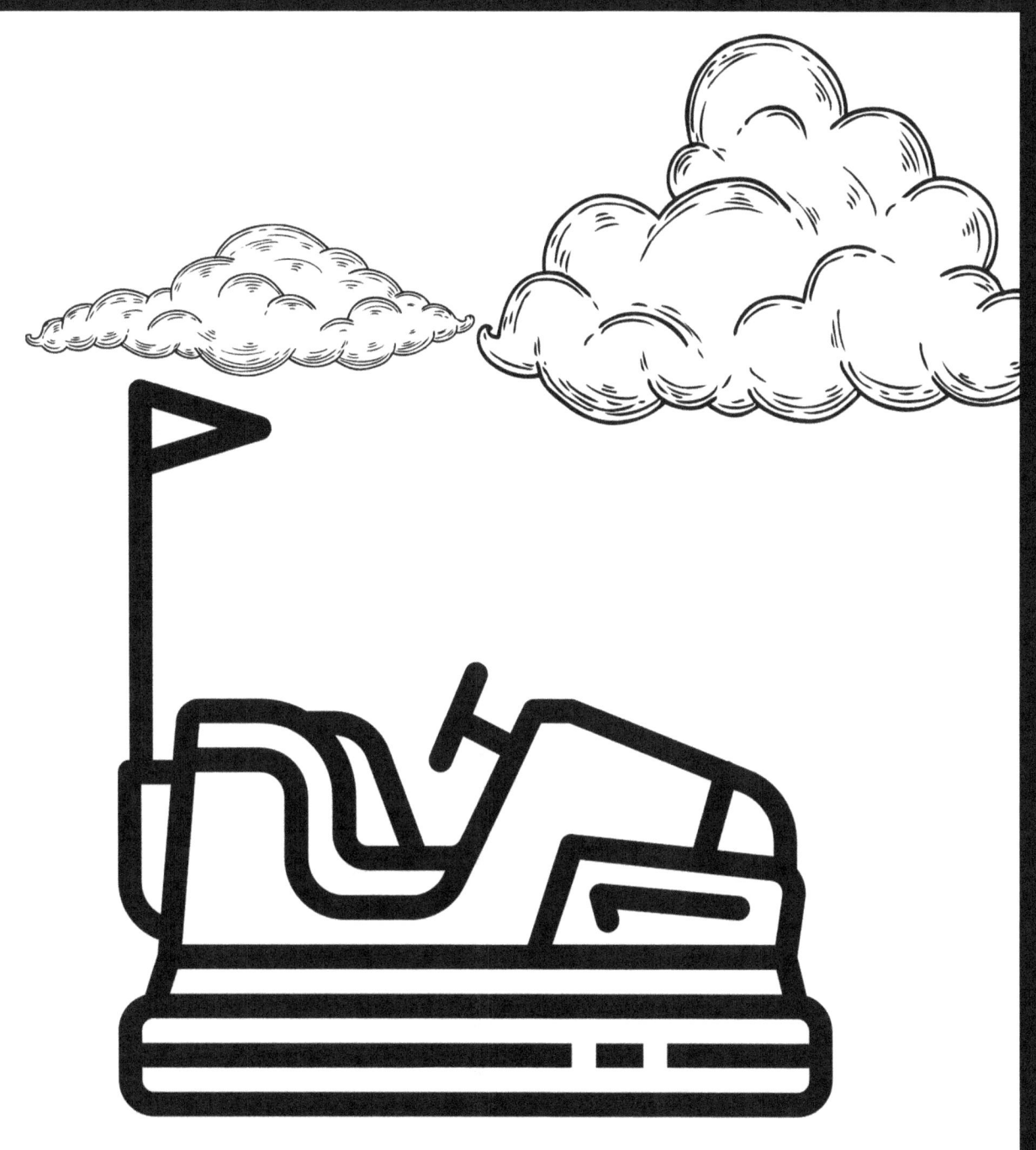

Relax

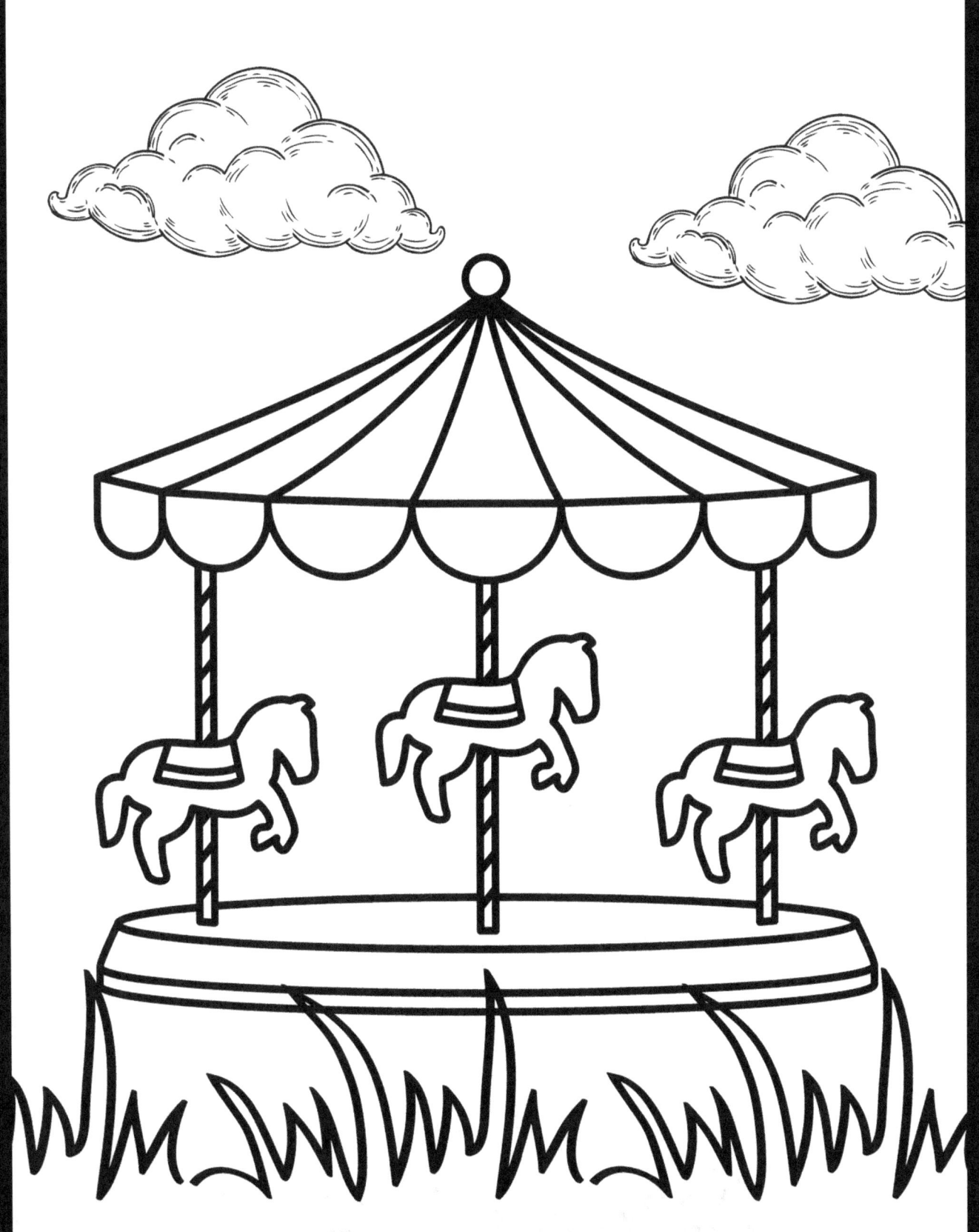

Circus Days

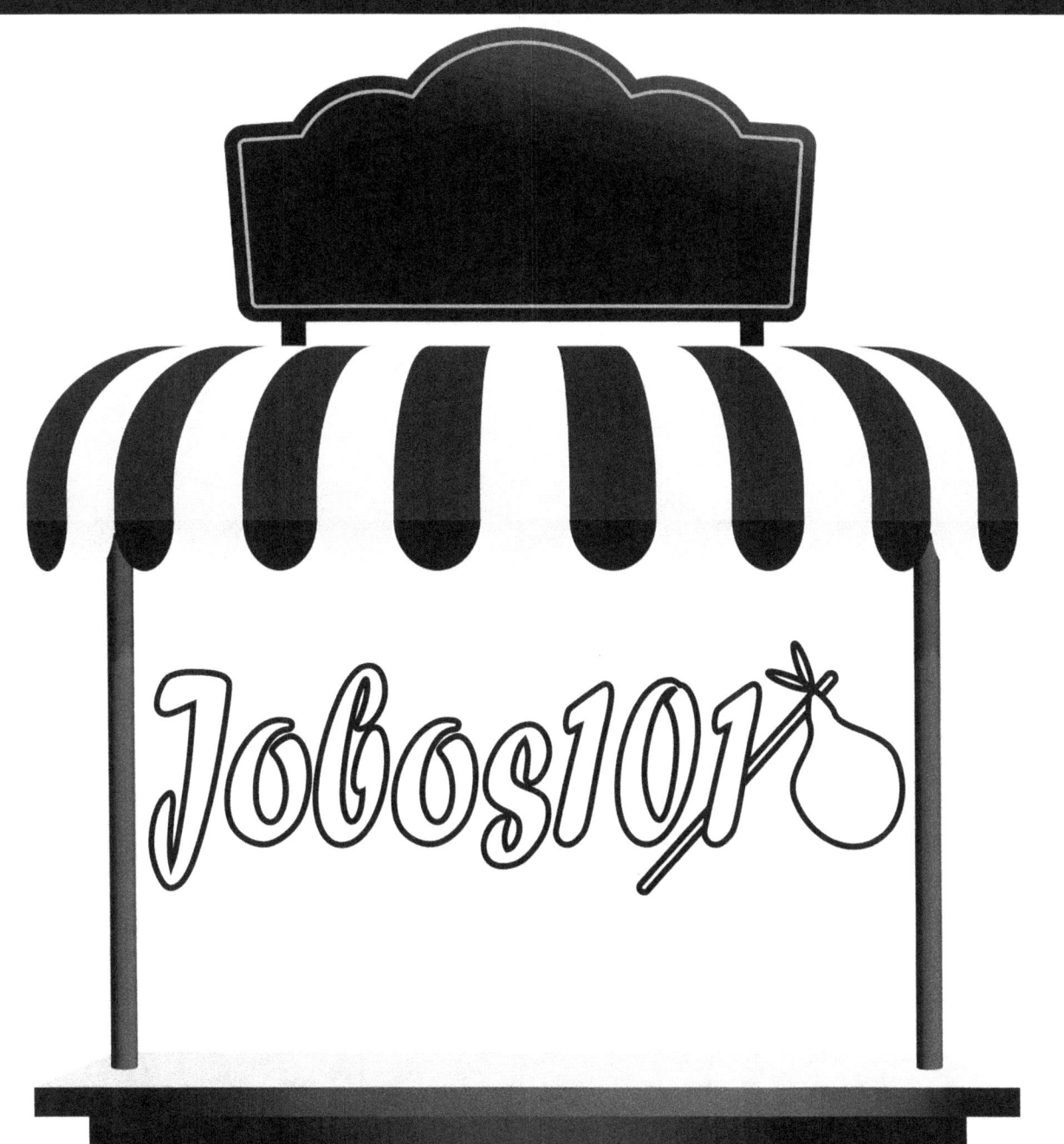

Jobos101

www.ingramcontent.com/pod-product-compliance
Lightning Source LLC
Chambersburg PA
CBHW080441220526
45465CB00007B/2719